Soul Stir-lings of a Sister in Christ

Cassandra K. James

SOUL STIR-LINGS OF A SISTER IN CHRIST

Copyright @ 2025

Cassandra K. James

All right reserved

ISBN : 9780-5783-5877-2

No parts of this book may be reproduced in any written, electronic recording, or photocopied form without written permission from the publisher or author.

This book was written in the United States of America

Published by Soul Stirrings LLC

For all orders for books or writing a review; via email@

SoulStirrings1@gmail.com

For all other inquiries, contact the author via email:
Seemyopic50@gmail.com

Free images by upsplash.com

Dedication

I would like to dedicate this book to my beloved sons, Curbris, Jamie, and Terrence, and to my family. May you always live a Christ-like life and return with honor.

CJ

Acknowledgment

This book is a gift from Heavenly Father, meant to encourage and uplift each person who receives a copy. May you continue to be blessed always! Thank you to every friend and family member for your support always.

Table Of Contents

Dedication 2

Acknowledgment 3

My Dearest Sister in Christ 5

Why am I here? 7

Happy, Happy, Birthday 8

I am a child of an awesome God! 10

Because I'm not perfect 12

Dear Heavenly Father! 14

Oh Lord, will thy hear my prayer? 15

Where is my Heavenly Father? 16

Psalm 23rd Poem 18

Mo-Ma 20

Scriptural References in the Poem 22

Appendix 23

About Author 23

My Dearest Sister in Christ

Oh, how I truly love you with every fiber of my being.
I love you to the highest hills, the very staircase to heaven,
where love abounds and souls are found.

The thought of offending my sister in Christ hurts me to my core—
so deep.
It's like losing a dear friend, and now I weep.
My heart aches for your care in Christ!
For in as much as you have done it to the least of my brethren, you
have done it to me. (Matthew 25:40)

Of course, I am not perfect, as Jesus Christ was.
For that purpose, we all need forgiveness—just because.
I had no right to say anything right or wrong!

Could you find it in your heart to forgive me? It's been too long.

I miss my dearest sister in Christ, whom I have loved for a short time but very strong.
For this reason, I beg the Lord to not let this string alone.
Living in the Gospel without my dearest sister seems so unfair.
I have learned my lesson. I know not, nor dare, to offend another or not care.

I hope and pray you know I love you, my dearest sister, and I declare
that even if it takes a lifetime, in thought, I will always be there.
How long will it be?
I hope not long to rekindle a friendship between you and me.

For I know that there is a God above,
who hears us when we cry in love.
Asking Heavenly Father to soften one's heart,
and give us a blessing in spirit to make up and never part.

We can search near or far,
but the same troubles will be where we are.
Until we return to heal the pain,
this will eat at us and remain.

Please know I hold your friendship dear,
and my love for you will always be here.

—@CJ (aistitnojca-amen)

Why am I here?

I am here because there is a plan for me!
It's called the plan of salvation, and it's the key.

Why am I here?
I came here with a body, designed in God's likeness and image.
(Gen. 5:1)
To help prepare the world, to help their lineage.

Why am I here?
I am here to help gather Israel, come to the fold,
So I don't have much time because I am getting old.

—@CJ *(aistitnojca-amen)*

Happy, Happy, Birthday

Happy, happy birthday, it's _____'s day!
    May you enjoy your date of birth and not overplay.

    Happy, happy birthday, he/she is so kind,
The Lord blessed him/her with skills that come right on time.

Happy, happy birthday, he/she is a renowned _____.
    During life's duty, to serve and protect life's needs, like a
    _____.

    Happy, happy birthday, it is therapeutic what he/she does.
        I dare you to try him/her—just because.

    Happy, happy birthday! He/she leaves you nourished,
        Happy to return for a relief you'll cherish.

Happy, happy birthday! At age _____, shows lots of love,
From God, who is in heaven above.

Happy, happy birthday! May you have fun today,
And may COVID-19 and the pandemic go away.

Happy, happy birthday!

—@CJ *(aistitnojca-amen)*

I am a child of an awesome God!

Who whispers to my spirit to do good and be odd.
He loves me like You, {Man}, but I say, "Nay,
The meek will He guide in judgment and teach His way." *(Psalm 25:9)*

I was given this time to come forth,
Amid many trials and afflictions, thenceforth.
Fear not! Yea, though I walk through the valley of the shadow of death,
I will fear no evil, for Thou art with me, *(Psalm 23:4)* till my last breath.

I strive unceasingly to do His will,
Although there are evils lurking to get their thrills.
Oh yes, I have an awesome God!
He fights my battles and beats all odds.

Elohim is His name, and obedience is the game.
When my enemies attack me from all sides,
The Holy Ghost comes in to protect and guide.

There is a God who hears my cries,
Who will fight against evil to prevent my demise.
There is a God, and if you dare,
Try Him out against Satan's snares.

I know that there is a God—
He loves me and understands me.
He knows my heart and what I am capable of.

With that said, I believe He will never leave me alone,
Even if the world shuts me out and declares that I am unknown.
I truly believe it will be better,
No matter what the weather.

I trust in every word that proceeds out of His mouth.
I am His child—no doubt.
Most of all, He has always kept His promises with us.
I can trust Him, no matter what's up!

—@CJ *(aistitnojca-amen)*

Because I'm not perfect

As a sister, sometimes I lose track.
Of what friendship really means and what it is to get back.

Because I am not perfect,
I forget to pardon persons or offense,
While jumping ahead and pulling up my defense.

Because I'm not perfect,
I fail sometimes at being a friend.
Can we just forgive each other
And put this pettiness to an end?

Because I'm not perfect,
I read, *"Father, forgive them, for they know not what they do."*

(Luke 23:34)
For with that same mercy, He extends it to you.

Because I'm not perfect,
I have to pray to be slow to anger and appease the strife,
While being grateful to live and love others in life.

Because I'm not perfect,
It is said your teeth and tongue may fall out,
But you still get along—without a doubt.

Because I'm not perfect,
We all will have discomfort in relationships, etc., at times.
So let us pray to Thee for strength and unity to clear our minds.

Because I'm not perfect,
I am one to repent of sins against our Lord and Savior,
And He remembers them no more—nor the intent.

Because I'm not perfect,
I come with a humble heart to plead for forgiveness,
And pray for two Sisters in Christ to gather, makeup,
And never part.

—@CJ *(aistitnojca-amen)*

Dear Heavenly Father!

Please give me strength and wisdom this day,
To do the things You want me to, without the slightest delay.
To find courage with conviction,
With little or no restriction.

To fight for righteousness and blessings,
The choice ones that may be pressing.
I ask of Thee humbly now,
To show mercy on me somehow—
In troubled times,
And allow me to find Favor to endow.

And may the Lord Jesus Christ grant our prayers,
Answered according to our faith *(Mosiah 27:12-14)*,
And may Satan be blocked by his own snares.

—@CJ *(aistitnojca-amen)*

Oh Lord, will thy hear my prayer?

I am in sorrow, and I need Thy care.
I don't know what to do or where to go.
Could You show me—in the spirit or so?

I feel I don't have the strength to go through much more,
For my mind and body are in such an uproar.
Worry and anxiety have me in despair.
Lord, are You there, and are You aware?

Is it true that You carry me,
Like footsteps in the sand?
When I am in bondage or I need a hand,
Oh Lord, wilt Thou hear my prayer?

For I'm in a world that is so unfair.
Oh Lord of hosts, blessed is the man that trusteth in Thee, *(Psalms 84:12)*.
Oh yes, He hears my prayers and answers with a guarantee.

—@CJ *(aistitnojca-amen)*

Where is my Heavenly Father?

It is so hard to keep the faith and know there is a God,
When you raise your hands, your heart, and soul to the Lord—and in being the odd.
And in return, you hear, you see, you feel nothing but emptiness,
And the longer you suffer, the more you have bitterness.

I have cried, prayed, and begged till I am numb;
I feel like a fool, and now I am dumb.
Where is my Heavenly Father, who promised to answer my prayers?
Or is He a figure of my imagination or something in the air?

"Did I not speak peace to your mind concerning the matter?
What greater witness can you have than from God?" (D&C 6:23)
Or do you choose Satan, the latter?

If He answers yes, confidence you will gain.
If He says no, He prevents error, and there you will remain.
When answers to immediate prayers don't come right away,
We may misunderstand the truths of prayer and lose our way.

To get blessings from the Lord, we have to obey,
Basic principles like faith and trust in Him—or we will stray,
Or even betray,
The very One we love and can't do without—
Our Lord and Savior, Jesus Christ, without a doubt.

—@CJ *(aistitnojca-amen)*

Psalm 23rd Poem

I was told by the Spirit of the Lord, who watches attentively over me,
That I needed not to want, because Jesus was sent for us as a Shepherd for free.

When I was instructed to lie down yet in green pastures,
A thought came to me: *"Be still, my child,"* as a stone is set without a gesture.
He then guided me beside still waters, to keep me safe and in order,
Reestablishing my soul while directing my path in gold,
Teaching me righteousness to never forsake the gospel of Jesus Christ.

Amen; always for His name's sake.

Though I walk through a valley, seeing a shadow of death,
I won't fear evils, even down to my last breath.
While Thy rod protects and guides, God comforts, instructs, and abides.

A place is set in the house of the Lord for me.
Whatever is bound on earth is bound in heaven and will be.
For no unclean thing can enter God's eternal rest.
There will be many to come and few to stay and do their best.

Thou anointest my head the very hour;
The Lord blesses me with assurance through the priesthood power.
Where much is given, much is expected.
Lengthen your stride, but don't become neglected.

As a cup runs over or spills, the Lord may tell us to be still.
As we follow the Lord in goodness, not running faster than we can,
Let us rest between some madness and stick to Heavenly Father's plan.

(Psalm 23)

—@CJ *(aistitnojca-amen)*

Mo-Ma

When I think of a song that my sons sang to me,
It brings me to a humble place, sweet yet on my knees.
It gives me great pleasure to know that the Lord was the key!
I couldn't do it alone without a companion, as you can see!

Honor thy father and thy mother; that thy days may be long upon the land,
{Exodus 20:12} always remember that Heavenly Father is there, to instruct and lend a hand.
My sons stand up and call me blessed among women on the last day.
The love and respect they have for me, I believe, will never decay.

Having sons was a great joy, valued with a life of learning.
I was told to teach them to be boys to men and also to make an

honest earning.
I was blessed, moreover, to teach them to pray, always trusting in Thee.
So, when they die, if they live worthily, they could go to the highest degree.

So, the song is called "Ma-ma,"
I'm taken into the body as nourishment to the soul.
It depicts a real lady with faith and trust in Thee as a whole.
I fought for my young until they grew old, raising them to be upstanding and honourable—that was the goal.

Even when times got a bit rough, I gave my very last so it would be enough.
I hope they know I love them all with every Fiber of my being,
And I always pray to the Lord for their safety and well-being.

Now that I am older, almost on bended knee,
My sons all gather with families—number of 3—to give tribute to their mother on Mother's Day.
By singing that sweet, loving song called, 'Ma-ma, we love you. Hurrah!'

—@CJ *(aistitnojca)*

Scriptural References in the Poem

Matthews 25:40
Gen 5.1
Psalms 25:9
Psalms23:4
Luke23:34
Mosiah 27:12-14
Psalms84:12
D@C6:23
Psalm 23
Ex:20:12

Appendix

Whenever the reader sees one of Cassandra's poems, there is something at the end that means a lot to her:

NOTE: @ CJ {aistitnojca amen}

It is important to her to do and say everything so it is blessed in Heavenly Father's name.

It is an acronym for "and I say this in the name of Jesus Christ, Amen."

We hope you enjoyed Cassandra's insights of Faith, Family and Friendship!

About Author
Cassandra K. Jam

Cassandra K. James is a lady from the south. She is a mother, a grandmother, and a graduate. Through trials and tribulations, she has searched her soul to find ways to express herself in writing.

www.ingramcontent.com/pod-product-compliance
Lightning Source LLC
Chambersburg PA
CBHW042046290426
44109CB00001B/47